AF225306

WOMOAN

Copyright © 2019 AMF Media

All rights reserved.

Published by Talisman,

An imprint of AMF Media Ltd, 2019

No parts of this publication may be reproduced, stored in a retrieval system, or transmitted in any form or by any means, electronic, mechanical, photocopying, recording, or otherwise, without the prior written permission of the copyright owner.

This book is sold subject to the condition that it shall not, by way of trade or otherwise, be lent, resold, hired out, or otherwise circulated without the publisher's prior consent in any form of binding or cover other than that in which it is published and without a similar condition including this condition being imposed on the subsequent purchaser. Under no circumstances may any part of this book be photocopied for resale.

This is a work of fiction. Any similarity between the characters and situations within its pages and places or persons, living or dead, is unintentional and coincidental.

ISBN 978-1-9161181-3-3

WOMOAN™ and WO-MOAN™ are trademarked

You don't need facts to

WOMOAN™

A notebook for over privileged women desperately trying to find something that oppresses them.

Remember you don't need facts to WOMOAN

Remember you don't need facts to WOMOAN

Remember you don't need facts to WOMOAN

Remember you don't need facts to WOMOAN

Remember you don't need facts to WOMOAN

Remember you don't need facts to WOMOAN

Remember you don't need facts to WOMOAN

Remember you don't need facts to WOMOAN

Remember you don't need facts to WOMOAN

Remember you don't need facts to WOMOAN

Remember you don't need facts to WOMOAN

Remember you don't need facts to WOMOAN

Remember you don't need facts to WOMOAN

Remember you don't need facts to WOMOAN

Remember you don't need facts to WOMOAN

Remember you don't need facts to WOMOAN

Remember you don't need facts to WOMOAN

Remember you don't need facts to WOMOAN

Remember you don't need facts to WOMOAN

Remember you don't need facts to WOMOAN

Remember you don't need facts to WOMOAN

Remember you don't need facts to WOMOAN

Remember you don't need facts to WOMOAN

Remember you don't need facts to WOMOAN

Remember you don't need facts to WOMOAN

Remember you don't need facts to WOMOAN

Remember you don't need facts to WOMOAN

Remember you don't need facts to WOMOAN

Remember you don't need facts to WOMOAN

Remember you don't need facts to WOMOAN

Remember you don't need facts to WOMOAN

Remember you don't need facts to WOMOAN

Remember you don't need facts to WOMOAN

Remember you don't need facts to WOMOAN

Remember you don't need facts to WOMOAN

Remember you don't need facts to WOMOAN

Remember you don't need facts to WOMOAN

Remember you don't need facts to WOMOAN

Remember you don't need facts to WOMOAN

Remember you don't need facts to WOMOAN

Remember you don't need facts to WOMOAN

Remember you don't need facts to WOMOAN

Remember you don't need facts to WOMOAN

Remember you don't need facts to WOMOAN

Remember you don't need facts to WOMOAN

Remember you don't need facts to WOMOAN

Remember you don't need facts to WOMOAN

Remember you don't need facts to WOMOAN

Remember you don't need facts to WOMOAN

Remember you don't need facts to WOMOAN

Remember you don't need facts to WOMOAN

Remember you don't need facts to WOMOAN

Remember you don't need facts to WOMOAN

Remember you don't need facts to WOMOAN

Remember you don't need facts to WOMOAN

Remember you don't need facts to WOMOAN

Remember you don't need facts to WOMOAN

Remember you don't need facts to WOMOAN

Remember you don't need facts to WOMOAN

Remember you don't need facts to WOMOAN

Remember you don't need facts to WOMOAN

Remember you don't need facts to WOMOAN

Remember you don't need facts to WOMOAN

Remember you don't need facts to WOMOAN

Remember you don't need facts to WOMOAN

Remember you don't need facts to WOMOAN

Remember you don't need facts to WOMOAN

Remember you don't need facts to WOMOAN

Remember you don't need facts to WOMOAN

Remember you don't need facts to WOMOAN

Remember you don't need facts to WOMOAN

Remember you don't need facts to WOMOAN

Remember you don't need facts to WOMOAN

Remember you don't need facts to WOMOAN

Remember you don't need facts to WOMOAN

Remember you don't need facts to WOMOAN

Remember you don't need facts to WOMOAN

Remember you don't need facts to WOMOAN

Remember you don't need facts to WOMOAN

Remember you don't need facts to WOMOAN

Remember you don't need facts to WOMOAN

Remember you don't need facts to WOMOAN

Remember you don't need facts to WOMOAN

Remember you don't need facts to WOMOAN

Remember you don't need facts to WOMOAN

Remember you don't need facts to WOMOAN

Remember you don't need facts to WOMOAN

Remember you don't need facts to WOMOAN

Remember you don't need facts to WOMOAN

Remember you don't need facts to WOMOAN

Remember you don't need facts to WOMOAN

Remember you don't need facts to WOMOAN

Remember you don't need facts to WOMOAN

Remember you don't need facts to WOMOAN

Remember you don't need facts to WOMOAN

Remember you don't need facts to WOMOAN

Remember you don't need facts to WOMOAN

www.ingramcontent.com/pod-product-compliance
Lightning Source LLC
Chambersburg PA
CBHW080521030726
47592CB00012B/3430

* 9 7 8 1 9 1 6 1 1 8 1 3 3 *